Snitch

Norah McClintock

orca soundings

ORCA BOOK PUBLISHERS

Library and Archives Canada Cataloguing in Publication

McClintock, Norah
Snitch / written by Norah McClintock.

(Orca soundings)
ISBN 10: 1-55143-484-9 / ISBN 13: 978-1-55143-484-1

I. Title. II. Series.

PS8575.C62S63 2005   jC813'.54   C2005-904829-8

First published in the United States, 2005
Library of Congress Control Number: 2005930530

Summary: After his best friend snitches on him,
Josh must learn to control his anger.

Orca Book Publishers gratefully acknowledges the support for its
publishing programs provided by the following agencies: the Government
of Canada through the Book Publishing Industry Development Program
and the Canada Council for the Arts, and the Province of British Columbia
through the BC Arts Council and the Book Publishing Tax Credit.

Cover design by John van der Woude
Cover photography by FirstLight

Orca Book Publishers   Orca Book Publishers
PO Box 5626, Stn. B   PO Box 468
Victoria, BC Canada   Custer, WA USA
v8R 6s4   98240-0468

www.orcabook.com
Printed and bound in Canada.
Printed on 100% PCW recycled paper.
11 10 09 08 • 6 5 4 3

To dogs running free.

Chapter One

It was supposed to be easy. You choose, they had told me. You can either go to a regular anger management program, which is where, basically, you sit around with a bunch of losers once a week and talk about what makes you mad and what you could have done instead of punching out a wall or maybe a person. Or you can go to this special program where they teach you how to train dogs. Gee, let me think about it—door number one or door number two…

I went with the dogs. It had to be better than sitting around listening to a bunch of tantrum freaks gripe, right? Besides, how hard could it be?

Things went sour right from minute one.

The woman at the front desk told me to go to the room that she called the training room. I opened the door. And there was Scott. He was standing in the middle of the room with some other guys. He turned when the door opened. When he saw me he grinned, as if nothing had happened, as if we were still friends. He had a kind of lopsided smile that always made him look goofy. I didn't smile back at him. My hands curled into fists.

"Hey, Josh," said someone behind me.

I spun around, thinking it was some other guy from my past. Why not? With Scott there, things were already bad. They might as well get worse.

But it was Mr. "Call-me-Brian" Weller, who was in charge of the program. I'd met him once, just after I applied. That was part of the thing with this program. You had to go to an interview before they let you in. Mostly they asked questions about your experience with animals—whether you had ever had any pets, whether you liked animals, what you thought of people who hurt animals. I'd admitted that I had never had a pet and that I wasn't sure how much I liked animals. I figured that would be the end of it—they'd ship me off to the regular program. But they didn't.

Mr. Weller smiled at me. "Did you manage to find the place all right?" he asked.

"My brother drove me," I said. I live with my older brother Andrew, his wife Miranda, and their kid Digby (don't get me started on what kind of dumb name that is), who is nine months old.

"It's nice to have a big brother who's so supportive," Mr. Weller said.

Mostly Andrew was glad I was in the program because it would keep me out of the apartment for a couple more hours. I had been living with him and Miranda for nearly a month now, ever since I got out of the group home. Miranda never came out and said she didn't want me there, but I could tell she wasn't thrilled. The place was so small. She and Andrew shared a bedroom with Digby and his crib. I slept on the couch in the living room/dining room. Besides those two rooms, the apartment had a kitchen and a bathroom. Andrew said I could live there as long as I didn't mess up again. He said that as soon as I finished with the program, I had to get a job—sooner if I could swing it. But that was going to be hard because I was going to school in the mornings to make up for at least a couple of the classes I had messed up last year, and the teacher really piled on the homework. Andrew said I'd have to work all summer and keep a part-time job when school started so that I could contribute to the household. He said as soon as I got a job and proved that I could hold it, he would start looking for a bigger place.

I looked at Scott again. He seemed right at home with the other guys. Mr. Weller looked at him too.

"You and Scott know each other, don't you?" he said. He asked it like it was a question. But I knew he had read my file. So I knew he already had the answer.

"Don't worry about it, Josh," he said. "If it turns out to be a problem for you that Scott is here, we can deal with it."

Right. Like I needed someone to handle my problems for me. I took another look at Scott and said, "Why should it be a problem?"

Mr. Weller looked at me for a moment. Then he nodded and held out a hand, a signal to me that I should go right on in.

There were three rows of chairs set up, each row with eight chairs in it. But when I counted, there were only fourteen people in the room, including Mr. Weller. Only one was a girl. She went right over to Mr. Weller the minute he came into the room, so I figured she was a helper. She was kind of cute.

Scott went up to her and said something. She laughed. Scott could be so charming. At least, that's the impression he liked to give. But I wasn't buying it. Then Scott looked at the back of the room where I was standing. He grinned at me again. I gave him my frozen look, the one that said, *I don't care*. But inside I knew I did care. I was going to get even with him if it was the last thing I did.

Chapter Two

Mr. Weller told everyone to take a seat. Twelve of us did. I expected the girl to stay up front with Mr. Weller, and Scott to sit down with the rest of the guys. I was going to tell him to get lost if he tried to sit anywhere near me. But he didn't. Scott stayed up front with Mr. Weller. The girl sat down with the rest of us. Another person had come into the room—a middle-aged woman. She looked like a teacher or a librarian.

"You all know me," Mr. Weller said. He told us—again—that we could just call him Brian. He told us that learning to train dogs would teach us a lot about ourselves. He said that dogs are like little kids—they respond well to patience and kindness, and they don't respond well to anger. Then he introduced us to the woman. Her name was Maggie—"Just Maggie will do," she said. She was the dog trainer. I still couldn't figure out what Scott was doing up there.

Then Maggie said, "And this is Scott. He's my assistant."

I stared at Scott. He was standing up there, beaming at us all as if being an assistant dog trainer made him someone special. Maybe some of the guys in the room thought so too. But that's because they didn't know Scott like I did. They didn't know what he had done.

"In a few minutes," Maggie said, "you will be introduced to your animals. But before we bring them in, you need to understand your responsibility."

A couple of guys groaned when they heard that word. Sometimes it seemed like the only word that adults knew. Andrew used it a lot. "I have responsibilities now, Josh," he'd say. Or "One day you'll be responsible for someone besides yourself. Then you'll see what it's like, Josh." He made it sound like responsibility was a cranky old gorilla that you had to carry on your back forever.

According to Maggie, it was up to us what happened to the dogs that were in the program with us. She said they all had serious behavior problems. She said that because of their problems, the animal shelter wasn't able to put them up for adoption. We were going to work with them to help them overcome their problems. If we were successful, the dogs would be able to find real homes. If we failed ... She shrugged and then she smiled and said she knew if we were patient and worked hard, we wouldn't fail.

After Maggie finished talking, she asked if there were any questions.

No one put up a hand. No one said anything.

If Maggie was disappointed that no one asked anything, she didn't show it. She told us that the dogs in the program weren't vicious. She said we shouldn't be afraid of them. She told us how to greet a strange dog—don't look them straight in the eyes the first time you met them (dogs see this as threatening), don't smile at them (a dog sees this as baring your teeth, which, to dogs, is threatening), don't rush directly to the dog (also threatening), don't pat the dog on the head...I began to wish I was in a regular program. I understood guys with anger management problems. I didn't know anything about dogs. And I didn't like what I was hearing.

Maggie nodded to Scott. He left the room. When he came back, there were three other people with him. Each of them was holding onto four dog leashes. Each leash had a dog at the end. Most of the dogs were barking and growling and jumping around. A couple of the dogs were pulling in the opposite direction, like all they wanted to do was get out of the room.

Some of the guys looked at each other. I bet some of them were thinking the same thing I was—no wonder those dogs couldn't get adopted. They were like hyperactive kids, yapping and jumping and not paying any attention to Scott and the other people who were trying to get them to calm down.

"Okay," Mr. Weller said. "I am going to call your names. When you hear your name, come up and meet your dog."

One by one, guys got up and walked to the front of the room. Nobody seemed in a big hurry to get there. A couple of guys walked with more confidence. Maybe they had dogs at home. One guy must not have been paying attention to Maggie. As soon as he got to the front of the room, he stuck out his hand in front of the dog he was supposed to be training. The dog lunged at his hand. The guy jumped back so fast he got tangled up in a chair in the front row. He fell over. Everyone laughed.

Finally there were only two dogs left. One was a small hairy thing. I don't even know what kind it was. It was one of the dogs that had been pulling to get out of the room. The other was a big white dog that looked like a cross between a pit bull and something even nastier. I looked at the girl. We were the only two people whose names hadn't been called. Then Mr. Weller said, "Amy." The girl got up and walked slowly to the front of the room as if she were walking to the electric chair or something. She was probably scared she was going to get the big dog.

Of course, she didn't.

No, they gave her the little dog, whose name was Coco. They saved the big one for me.

"Josh," Mr. Weller said, "meet Sully."

I did everything that Maggie had said to do and didn't do anything that she had warned us not to. It didn't make any difference. Sully took one look at me and lunged. The guy who had been holding his leash was asleep on the job or something because he let go, and all of a sudden this dog was jumping on me. He was growling. All I saw was teeth and drool. I froze. Then someone had hold of the leash again and was talking to the dog in a soft, firm voice, telling it to "Get down. Down, boy."

It was Scott.

He didn't look the least bit afraid.

Once he got the dog calmed down, he brought it over to me and stayed with me until the dog stopped jumping around. I wanted to tell him to get lost, but I didn't want to get stuck alone with the dog. What a monster.

Chapter Three

"So, how was it?" Andrew said. He was waiting for me out in the parking lot. He had come directly from work. His main job was shift manager at a video store. He still had on his store T-shirt. He had a second job delivering newspapers. He did that between 3:30 and 5:30 in the morning.

"What do you think?" I said. I got into the car and slammed the door. I had spent half an hour with that stupid dog. Most of the time Scott was right there with me because it turned out—*of course*—that my dog had more problems than any of the other dogs in the program.

"Yeah, but dogs," Andrew said. "That should be fun, right? Remember when you were little? You always wanted a dog."

I'd been mad, too, that I had never got one. My dad always said they were more trouble than kids, and kids were trouble enough. The only kind of animal my dad liked was fish—at the end of his fishing line. My main memory of my dad is going fishing with him. Hauling in a fish and dropping it into the bottom of his old boat and bashing its brains in with the weighted wooden fish basher he called a priest. My dad was calm and happy when he was in his boat with some beer and some bait. And because he was happy, I was happy.

After Andrew figured out that I didn't want to talk about the program, he put on some music. I closed my eyes and pretended to sleep until we got home.

The whole building smelled like food, even the elevator. I could pick out the smell of onions and garlic and curry and chicken. Some people think it stinks, especially the curry smell, but not me. Those smells always make my mouth water.

When the elevator opened on the eighth floor, where Andrew's apartment is, Daryl Matheson pushed his way in while Andrew and I were trying to get out. Daryl, lives at the opposite end of the hall from Andrew. Andrew doesn't like him. He says guys like Daryl who spend all their time just hanging around, are on their way to nowhere, probably via the prison system.

Daryl smirked at me when I stepped around him to get out of the elevator.

"You got the worst stuff I ever saw," he said. "Nothing even worth stealing."

I couldn't figure out what he was talking about until I saw what was sitting in the hall outside Andrew's apartment door. It was a wooden crate with my name painted on the side.

"Hey!" I said. I'd had that crate forever. My dad had made it for me and had stenciled my name on it. It was heaped high with my stuff—clothes and CDs and a bunch of my other things. "What's this doing out here?"

Andrew unlocked the apartment door. I scooped up the crate and followed him inside. Miranda was standing in the kitchen, a magazine open on the counter in front of her. Great, she was going to try another recipe. She was always trying new recipes, most of them vegetarian, and they were always terrible.

"What was my stuff doing out in the hall?" I said.

"You're lucky the baby's been cranky all day," Miranda said. "Otherwise it would be out back by the dumpster. I told you, Josh. You can't leave your stuff lying all over the living room. That's where I watch TV. That's where the baby plays."

"Yeah, but, jeez, it's my stuff. You can't just—"

Miranda reached into the box and pulled out my penknife. "The baby had this in his mouth," she said. She reached in again. "And yesterday I found him pounding on my new table with this." She held up the wood priest—what she preferred to call a fish club. She always made a sour face when she saw it. She thought it was barbaric to club fish. The priest had my initials on it. Well, really they were my dad's initials. But his name was Jack, so his initials were the same as mine.

Andrew shook his head when he saw it. "What do you even have that thing for?" he said.

"Dad gave it to me."

Andrew made a sour face. "If he'd given it to me, I'd have burned it a long time ago," he said. "I'd have burned anything he gave me, even thousand-dollar bills." He looked at the priest again. "I can't believe they gave that back to you."

I had to practically beg my youth worker, who finally managed to get it returned. I told him it was the only thing I had of my dad's.

"If it were me—" said Andrew. He stopped when I gave him a sharp look.

"What do you mean?" Miranda said. She had been engaged to Andrew at the time, so she knew I'd been in trouble. But she didn't know all the details.

"Nothing," I said. "Nothing, okay? And stay away from my stuff, Miranda, unless you want to find a box of your things out in the hall."

"Come on, Josh," Andrew said, trying to calm me down. Then the baby started wailing.

"I think he's cutting another tooth," Miranda said. "He's been crying all day. Go pick him up, Andrew." She did that a lot too—bossed Andrew around, told him, "Do this, do that," as soon as he got home from work. He never argued. He went into the living room, where a play-pen was crammed in between the sofa and the dining table. The baby yowled even louder when Andrew picked him up.

Miranda turned to me. "This is my place, Josh. I don't want it messy and I don't want the baby picking up things he shouldn't. You understand me?"

I opened the fridge.

"Stay out of there," she said. "We're going to have supper soon."

I reached inside for a piece of leftover chicken. Andrew went along with the vegetarian stuff, but he still insisted on meat once in a while. Miranda grabbed it out of my hand and shut the fridge door.

"I mean it, Josh." She was always saying that. "You're going to have to wait."

In the other room, the baby was still yowling. Jeez, what a place!

That night I heard Andrew and Miranda talking. If you ask me, Miranda planned it that way. She didn't even bother keeping her voice down.

"He can't stay here forever," she said. "He's rude. He never helps out."

"That's not true," Andrew said. "He's great with Digby."

"When he *wants* to be, which isn't very often. I love you, Andrew. And I know you feel responsible for Josh. But it's just not working out."

I expected Andrew to cave in to her like he always did. But instead he argued with her. He told her he *was* responsible for me. He told her that as soon as I finished the program, I was going to get a job and start to pay my own way. He told her I was trying hard to change. Then it got quiet. It didn't surprise me. Miranda was one of those people who clammed up when she didn't get her own way.

The bedroom door opened.

"Josh?" Andrew said, his voice low.

I pretended to be asleep. I heard him go into the kitchen. A little later I heard the apartment door open and then close again. In the bedroom, the baby started to cry.

Chapter Four

When we arrived at the program, we were supposed to go and see our dogs so they could get used to us. Then we went to the training room and spent forty-five minutes talking about what our day had been like so far. Mr. Weller said the idea was to decompress before Maggie and Scott got there and showed us how to train the dogs. He said the dogs could tell if we were tense or angry about something, but that if we talked out our problems first, we would be relaxed and that would relax the dogs. Maybe it would have worked, too, except that as soon as we settled in a circle in the training room, someone new joined us.

Travis Keenan.

He swaggered into the room, looking cool in his leather jacket, his hands jammed into the pockets. He looked around like he expected everybody to drop what they were doing and pay attention to him. That's the kind of guy he was. It didn't matter how big a room was, it was never big enough for Travis and his ego. He had a scar under one eye that made him look even meaner than he was.

Mr. Weller got up and got a chair for him, which probably made Travis feel even more special. Then we all had to say our names one by one and talk about the best thing and the worst thing that had happened to us so far that day. I said the best thing was coming up here to learn something new, even though that wasn't true. The actual best thing so far was getting out of the house so I didn't have to listen to Miranda nag at me. I said the worst thing hadn't happened yet, even though I couldn't think of anything worse than Travis being part of the group. Mr. Weller looked at me as if he didn't quite believe me, but he let it pass.

When we finished going round the circle, Mr. Weller told us to stack the chairs out of the way. Travis hooked his chair in one hand and started to drag it over to the wall. He paused when he got to me and said, "Don't think I've forgotten about you, Gillick." Then he stared at me, trying to scare me. Right.

Mr. Weller clapped his hands to get our attention. Some guy I had never seen before came into the room and stood next to Mr. Weller. He was holding a camera. Then Maggie and Scott and a couple of other people brought in the dogs. I was kind of hoping Sully, the big white dog from yesterday, had got sick or something. But, no, there he was, barking and straining at his leash. It was complete chaos for a few minutes until everyone got their dogs. I hung back as long as I could. Finally I had no choice. I took Sully by the leash. He barked and jumped up on me.

"Hey!" I said. "Stop. Bad dog."

The guy with the camera turned toward me. I realized he was videotaping me.

"Hey," I said. "Point that thing somewhere else." But I don't think he heard me because Sully was still barking and jumping up on me. Finally Scott came over, took the leash from me and talked gently but firmly to the dog. And, just like that, the dog calmed down. Figures, huh?

"He knows me," Scott said. "He'll be better when he gets to know you."

Maggie said we were going to start teaching the dogs how to obey commands. She said the goal was to get the dogs to obey the commands every single time. The first thing she showed us was how to get the dogs to sit. It sounded simple, especially when she demonstrated it with a dog she had brought with her. But guess what? It wasn't simple. Especially not with Sully.

The girl, Amy, got her mousy little dog to sit down almost right away. Her dog wasn't aggressive like most of the others. Her dog was terrified of people.

Most of the other guys got their dogs to sit at least once.

Even Travis finally got his dog to sit.

But me? My stupid dog just stood there, no matter how many times I followed Maggie's instructions. Finally I lost it. I shoved the dog's butt down onto the floor and told him to stay there. The dog's response: he jumped up, barking and growling, and tried to take a chunk out of me. When I jumped back out of his way, I stepped on Amy's dog's tail. The little dog yowled and bit my ankle—actually *bit* my ankle. Everyone thought that was hilarious. Well, except for Mr. Weller. He got Maggie to take my dog, and then he told Scott to take me to the first-aid room and have someone look at my ankle.

"I can find it myself," I said. No way was I going anywhere with Scott.

Mr. Weller looked at me, but he didn't argue. Instead he gave me directions.

The dog's sharp teeth had broken the skin. The woman who looked at the bite—she was young and had a terrific smile—said it wasn't deep and I shouldn't worry because the dog had had all her shots. She washed it and put some cream on and a Band-Aid on top of that.

When I went back into the room, Sully barked at me again. Stupid dog. Everyone laughed.

"Hey, Gillick," Travis said. "They got you on tape. Maybe we should send it to that funny video show on TV—what do you think?"

Everyone laughed again.

Andrew was waiting out in the parking lot. He looked tired. It had been late the night before when he went out, and I hadn't heard him come back in.

"How'd it go?" he said.

"You gonna ask me that every day?" I snapped.

"Whoa. Someone's in a bad mood."

I got in the car and slammed the door. Andrew got in beside me.

"That bad, huh?" he said, smiling, trying to keep it light.

"I hate it, okay?" I said. "I hate the stupid dogs. I hate the people there. I hate everything about it."

"Well, you're going to have to stick with it, Josh," he said. "You know that, right?"

"Yeah, I know. I have no choice. They're making me do it. But they can't make me like it."

Blam! Jeez, I just about jumped out of my seat. Andrew had brought both his fists down hard on the steering wheel. His face was all twisted. He looked like he wanted to punch something. He sat there, breathing hard, not moving. After about a minute, his breathing went back to normal.

"They called me in to work tonight,"

he said. "I'll drop you off, then I have to go."

Great. One crappy day followed by what was guaranteed to be a crappy night alone with Miranda.

Chapter Five

"Hurry up, Josh. You're going to be late," Miranda said for what was probably the hundredth time the next afternoon.

I was rooting in a pile of my stuff that was still in the crate that Miranda had threatened to throw out the other day. I knew there was a clean T-shirt in there somewhere. Digby had thrown strained carrots at the one I was wearing when I got home from school and I hadn't gotten around to taking all my dirty stuff down to the laundry room in the basement.

"Josh, did you hear me? You're going to be late."

Her voice was as high and irritating as a dentist's drill. I couldn't figure out how Andrew could stand it. I found a clean shirt—well, cleaner than the one I had on—and changed into it. I threw the stained one into the crate.

"You should do your laundry, Josh," Miranda said.

"I gotta go," I said. I hurried out of the apartment and spent five minutes waiting for the stupid elevator. It didn't come. So I ran down seven flights of stairs to the main floor.

I missed the bus by about two minutes, and the next one was late. By the time I got to the shelter, the session had already started. I headed for the door, but Scott blocked my way.

"You know the rules, Josh," he said. "If you're late, you have to wait for the break before you can go in. And then you have to apologize to everyone for not being on time."

Mr. Weller had told us that the first day. But that was none of Scott's business. I tried to push past him, but he grabbed my arm.

"What does it have to do with you?" I said. "You work with Maggie, not Brian."

"When you didn't show up on time, he asked me to watch for you and make sure you wait out here," Scott said. Boy, he really seemed to enjoy sticking it to me.

"This is all your fault, Scott," I said, my fists curling at my sides. "If it wasn't for you, I wouldn't even be here."

"And I have you to thank for my being here," Scott said. He said it like I had done him some kind of favor. That would be the day.

Twenty-five minutes later, I heard chairs scraping inside. The mid-meeting stretch. Scott opened the door to let me in.

"Josh, we were wondering what had happened to you," Mr. Weller said. I glanced around. Nobody else looked like they cared about me one way or the other.

After a few minutes, Mr. Weller clapped his hands to call the meeting back to order. Everyone sat down. Then Mr. Weller said, "I believe Josh has something to say." He looked at me. "Josh?"

Jeez, he was really going to make me do it.

"Sorry I'm late," I mumbled.

"We didn't hear you, Josh, did we?" Mr. Weller said.

Great. It was like being in kindergarten.

"I said, I'm sorry I was late," I repeated in a louder voice. "But my baby nephew threw some strained carrots at me and I had to find a clean shirt and the stupid elevator didn't come and—"

"Um, Brian," someone said. Travis. "Didn't you tell us that any apology that includes the word 'but' isn't really an apology, it's just an excuse?"

"I did say that," Mr. Weller said. He looked at me. "A sincere apology is just that—an apology. It doesn't include all kinds of justifications for being in the wrong."

Travis grinned at me.

Amy cleared her throat. "Sometimes it's really not a person's fault," she said in a quiet voice. "Sometimes you have a bad day when everything seems to go wrong."

"That's true too," Mr. Weller said. He turned to me. "But when you joined the program, Josh, you agreed to be here on time. Maybe if you'd aimed to get here a few minutes early instead of just on time, you wouldn't have missed the beginning of the session."

"Maybe if you didn't have that stupid rule about having to wait until the break, I wouldn't have had to stand out in the hall for the past twenty-five minutes," I said.

"Excuse me, Brian," Travis said, "but I don't think Gillick is making a sincere apology."

Mr. Weller looked at me. "Care to try that again, Josh?"

I apologized again. I didn't care whether it sounded sincere or not. Mr. Weller gave me a schoolteacher look. He told me to sit down and then moved on to the next part of the session.

Things didn't go much better after Maggie and Scott brought in the dogs. This time everyone got their dogs to sit at least once. Most of the dogs sat several times. But not Sully. He wouldn't listen to me.

"Stupid dog," I muttered, jerking on his leash.

Sully growled.

"He's tense," Scott said. Who had even asked him? "He's tense because you're tense. What you're feeling, Josh, it travels down the leash. If you want him to calm down and listen, you have to calm down. You can't make him do what you want by jerking his leash and yelling at him."

He took the leash from my hand and calmly told Sully to sit. It took him three tries, but he did it. Show-off. I wanted to hit him. But Mr. Weller was watching me, his arms crossed over his chest as if he was mad at me for not apologizing the way he wanted.

"Here," Scott said, handing the leash back to me. "Why don't you try? Just take a deep breath and think about something nice so you can calm down."

Mr. Weller was still watching me.

I thought about Digby and how he always looked so happy to see me when I got back to the apartment. Then I took a deep breath and tried to remember everything Maggie had told us about getting a dog to sit—what to say, how to move my hand. I did everything just like she had showed us.

Sully didn't sit.

"Your technique is good," Scott said. "Try it again."

I took another deep breath and started again.

I think I was the most surprised person in the room when Sully's butt finally hit the ground.

"Good dog," I said. "Good dog."

"There you go," Scott said. He flashed me his goofy, lopsided grin. "If he did it once, he can do it again. Let's reinforce what he's learned so he doesn't forget."

Sully sat again. And again. And again. He sat every single time I asked him to. I couldn't believe it.

"Good dog," I said, smiling at him. "Good dog."

Chapter Six

I could just about handle living in that cramped apartment when Andrew was home to distract Miranda. But lately he was pulling double shifts at the video store, on top of his second job delivering morning newspapers. That meant I was stuck with Miranda a lot. And she was always after me about something, sometimes the minute I came through the door.

Like the next day, when I came home after school to grab a bite to eat before I went to the program. She was in my face before I even closed the door.

"Did you think I wouldn't notice, Josh?" she screamed at me. "Do you think I'm that stupid?"

"I don't know what you're talking about." I tried to get past her and into the living room. But she blocked my way.

"What did you spend it on, Josh? Did you go to the arcade? Or maybe you hooked up with some of your old friends. Is that what you did?" She was so mad that she shoved me. And, boy, I don't like being shoved.

"What's your problem, anyway?" I said.

"I had forty-five dollars in my wallet this morning. It was for baby food and diapers. And it's gone."

Wait a minute.

"You think I stole money from you?"

"I don't think it, Josh. I know it. It was there this morning and now it's gone. And Digby sure didn't take it."

"Neither did I," I said. Andrew slipped me a few bucks every now and then. And I had this gig every Friday evening delivering a community newspaper. It didn't pay much, but it was enough for Cokes and fries every now and then.

"I'm telling Andrew," she said. She sounded just like a baby.

"You can tell him anything you want. I didn't take your money."

I pushed by her to go into the living room. And, okay, maybe I shoved her a little, to pay her back for pushing me. I turned on the TV.

She came into the room and snapped it off.

"You're not supposed to watch TV in the daytime," she said. "You're supposed to do your reading for school and then go to your program."

"I don't have any reading to do." It was a lie. My history teacher always assigned pages. But I didn't want to do anything just because she told me I had to.

"Then clean up this room," she said. "Your stuff is all over the place again."

I was about to tell her what I thought about her and her nagging when the apartment door opened.

"Hello?" Andrew called. He came into the living room.

"What are you doing home?" Miranda said.

"I'm not staying. I just stopped to give you this." He handed her some money. It looked like a couple of twenties and a five. Miranda stared at it.

"What's this for?" she said.

"I took some money out of your purse this morning."

Miranda stared at him. "You did?"

"To pay Rich. Remember when I blew that tire last week? Rich said he'd give me a deal on a retread if I paid cash. He came by this morning when I was on my way out. You were in the shower, so I took the money to pay him. I should have left you a note. But you said you weren't going out until this afternoon so no problem, right?"

"Right," she said.

"She accused me of stealing it," I said.

"What?" Andrew said.

"She was ragging on me for stealing it. She asked me if I was hooking up with my old friends."

Miranda's face turned red. "I was angry," she said lamely, to Andrew, not to me.

"Josh is doing great," Andrew said. "He wouldn't steal from you." He looked at me. "I'm really sorry, Josh."

"What are you sorry for? You didn't accuse me of being a thief. She did."

Andrew looked at Miranda. "I think you should apologize," he said quietly.

I could tell she didn't want to. She didn't even want to look at me.

"Come on, Miranda. You accused him of something he didn't do."

"I'm sorry," she said. She still wasn't looking at me. "But you have to admit, it was an understandable mistake."

"She's sorry," Andrew said.

"No she isn't. If she was sorry, she wouldn't be using the word 'but.' Mr. Weller says that 'but' turns an apology into a justification for being wrong."

Now Miranda looked at me, her eyes burning. "I said I was sorry," she said. She didn't sound sorry at all. She was angry at me. Again.

"You're sorry, all right," I said. "Sorry I live here. Sorry you have to look at me every day. Sorry I haven't messed up again so I'd be out of your life and this crappy little apartment."

"Josh—" Andrew said.

But I didn't want to listen to him, either. He was always making excuses for her. I pushed past both of them and left the apartment. I heard Andrew call my name, but I didn't stop. I ran all the way down the stairs to the ground floor and out the door.

"Hey," someone called. "Hey, look who it is."

I glanced over my shoulder. It was Travis. He was hanging out in the little park in front of my building with Daryl Matheson. Boy, it figured that those two knew each other. I kept right on going. I jumped on the first bus that came by.

I got to the shelter nearly an hour early. Mr. Weller was already in the training room. The chairs for the group had been set out in a circle, but Mr. Weller wasn't sitting there. He was sitting at a table on one side of the room. His briefcase was open on the floor beside him and he was reading a bunch of papers in file folders and making notes. He looked up when he saw me.

"Nice to see someone's actually taking my advice, even if you appear to be taking it to the extreme," he said, smiling. Boy, it was the first time I'd seen a smile that day. "Do me a favor?"

I shrugged. Why not? I didn't have anything else to do.

"Take this down to Maggie." He handed me a file folder. "You'll find her in the dog area. You think you can find that on your own?"

I nodded, even though I wasn't one hundred percent sure. The shelter is pretty big, with lots of hallways going off in all directions. I followed the signs and got lost a couple of times. Finally I heard barking. I walked toward the sound and found Maggie sitting at a little table at one end of the long hallway in the dog area. There were dog kennels on both sides, and the dogs all started barking when they saw me coming. Or maybe when they smelled me.

Maggie looked up and smiled. The second smile of the day.

"Brian asked me to give this to you," I said.

She took the folder and thanked me.

"Why don't you say hello to Sully while you're here?" she said. She handed me something. A treat for the dog.

"I don't know," I said. I was going to see him soon enough. And I had no idea if he was going to listen to me today or if he was going to ignore me and everyone was going to end up laughing at me again.

"He's lonely," she said. "They're all lonely. And dogs are social animals by nature. Go on."

I walked back down between the kennels until I came to Sully's. He was standing right at the entrance, which was like a gate in a chain-link fence.

"Hey, Sully," I said quietly. He wagged his tail. "Sit, boy."

To my complete astonishment, he dropped his butt down onto the ground.

"Good boy," I said. I slipped the treat through the gate into his mouth. He gulped it down and barked. Maybe I was wrong, but it sounded like a happy bark.

Chapter Seven

I felt pretty good—until I got back to the training room. Travis was standing right outside the door.

"Hey, Gillick," he said. "I see you're on time for a change."

I ignored him and went into the room. Mr. Weller wasn't there anymore.

"I bet you're surprised to see me here," Travis said. He had followed me inside and was standing close to me. He liked to stand close to people. He thought it scared them. "Bet you thought you'd got away from me, right?"

The best thing about getting out of the group home was getting away from Travis. He was a bully. He got kids into trouble all the time. He'd got me into trouble when I punched him out. The scar under his eye—that came from me. I wasn't sorry though. He deserved it for the way he was always picking on this one kid named Jonathan. He was only in the group home because he kept running away from the foster homes they put him in. Jonathan hardly ever talked and he cried a lot at night, so naturally Travis decided to give him a hard time.

I ignored him now.

"I know where you live," he said.

"Big deal." If he thought he was going to scare me, he was going to have to think again.

"I've seen your sister-in-law and that little baby. Cute kid, Gillick. Guess he takes after his mother's side of the family."

"You stay away from my place," I said.

Travis grinned. It made him look like even more of a snake than he was.

"I'm gonna get you," he said in a low singsong voice, tapping the scar under his eye. It was the same voice he used on Jonathan all the time. "For what you did, I'm gonna get you."

He sauntered across the room and took a seat in the circle of chairs. I decided to hang out outside the classroom until some more people got there. Scott was standing just outside the door.

"You can report him," he said.

"What?"

"Travis. You can report him for threatening you."

Scott had been listening. My life was none of his business, but he had been listening.

"I can handle it," I said.

"If he's hassling you, you can report him. You can get him kicked out of the program."

I just stared at him. "Yeah, I guess that's the way you'd handle it, right, Scott? You'd tell on him. But I'm not like you. I'm not a snitch."

I turned around to get away from him—and saw Amy standing right there behind me. She must have heard too. I felt like punching something.

After circle, Maggie and Scott brought in the dogs. Sully was rambunctious, as usual, but he didn't growl at me. He was wagging his tail, even when he jumped up on me.

We ran through the sitting exercise. Then Maggie told us we were moving on to the next step. We were going to teach the dogs how to lie down. Sully didn't catch on as fast as some of the other dogs, but by the end of the session, I'd got him to lie down twice. Maggie said that was real progress. I felt good for a change. I felt so good that I took a detour downtown on my way home. I went to a pet store and bought some treats for Sully.

That meant I got home later than I was supposed to.

Miranda was in the kitchen, working on supper. I thought maybe she'd apologize to me, but she didn't. Instead she said, "You're late. I was about to call Andrew at work."

"I had to make a stop."

"You're supposed to come right home." I couldn't believe it. She had accused me of something she knew I hadn't done, and she still wasn't apologizing to me. Instead she was mad at me all over again. "Clean up the living room."

I didn't move.

"Clean up the living room, Josh," she said again.

No way. She wasn't going to boss me around. I turned and walked out the door. I stayed out as long as I could, which wasn't that long. Andrew had told me when I went to live with him that I was supposed to be home by 9:00 every night. He said if I wasn't home, he would call my youth worker. If he did that, I'd be in trouble again.

The building Andrew lives in has a front entrance and a back entrance. Usually I go in the front way. But I didn't that night because when I got close to it, I saw that Daryl and a bunch of his friends were hanging around the door, hassling everyone who went in or out. I wasn't in the mood for that. I decided to go in the back way. It's a good thing I did because when I got to the back of the building, I saw it. My box. With my name on it and my stuff in it. Sitting right there on the ground next to the dumpster. I grabbed it and carried it upstairs.

When I got to the apartment, Miranda was sitting at the dining room table, clipping recipes out of a magazine and pasting them into a big binder. Digby was asleep in the bedroom. Miranda looked at the box and then at me.

"You're lucky you found it before the garbage truck got it," Miranda said. "I warned you. If you keep leaving your stuff lying around, I'm going to throw it out."

"If you touch my stuff again," I told her, "you'll be sorry."

"Don't talk to me like that, Josh."

"How would you like it if people did whatever they wanted with your stuff?" I said. I picked up the mug that was sitting in front of her—her special mug that no one was supposed to ever touch.

"Put that down," she said.

I raised it over my head. Boy, I was just aching to bounce it off the wall and watch it smash into a thousand pieces.

"Put it down, Josh."

I stared at her. Then I slammed it down on the table. It didn't break. I flopped onto the couch, where I wouldn't have to look at her, and turned on the TV. When she told me to do my homework, I turned it up louder. She got up and went into the bedroom. I heard her crying.

She must have called Andrew because when he came home, he didn't stop to talk to me. He went right into the bedroom. Maybe ten minutes later he came out again.

"You want to tell me your side?" he said.

"She threw my stuff out again. She has no right touching my stuff, Andrew."

"You're supposed to keep your stuff put away." He shook his head. "Come on, Josh, you made her cry."

"She started it," I said. "She always starts it."

"That's your big line, huh?" Andrew said. "She started it. She always starts it. *You* never start anything. You never finish anything, either. That's real mature, Josh."

"What do you mean, I never finish—"

"This is where I live, Josh. Miranda and Digby are my family. I want it to be a peaceful family. That means everybody, including you, has to live by the rules. If you make Miranda cry one more time, you're going to have to find someplace else to live. You hear me, Josh?" His face was all red and his hands were fists.

I couldn't remember the last time I had seen Andrew so angry.

Chapter Eight

Andrew was gone in the morning. The sink was filled with breakfast dishes. Miranda was in the bathroom, giving Digby a bath. I went to the fridge to get milk for my cereal. I hadn't slept well. I kept thinking about what Andrew had said. Miranda and Digby were his family. If I wanted to stay with them, I had to live by the rules.

If.

Where else would I go? A couple of the guys I knew from the group home had spent time on the street. Most of them went on about how great it was. But one guy, a guy the staff liked a lot and who kept to himself and spent most of his time reading or doing his homework, said they were full of it. He said life on the street was great if you wanted to eat junk food and try to keep clean by washing up in restaurant bathrooms. He said it was great if you didn't mind freezing your butt off under a pile of sleeping bags in an alley some place or bedding down in some squat that smelled like piss and some nights you were afraid to close your eyes because of the rats. Rats!

I filled the sink with water, squirted in some dish detergent and started to do the dishes. I was trying to do something good. As usual, it turned into something bad. I heard a noise behind me. When I turned, the mug I was holding slipped out of my hand and crashed onto the kitchen floor.

It was Miranda's favorite mug. The noise I had heard was Miranda, coming into the kitchen. She stared at the mug. It was in pieces on the floor.

"Thanks a lot, Josh," she said. Her face was crumpled up like she was going to cry. Over a stupid mug. "Do me a favor," she said. "From now on, don't touch anything that belongs to me."

I grabbed my school stuff and left the apartment. I wanted to slam the door—boy, did I want to. But I didn't.

It was good to finally get to the shelter. Sully didn't jump up on me at all. He wagged his tail and his bark sounded like he was laughing. He sat when he was supposed to. He lay down when he was supposed to. And for once he wasn't the last dog to learn the day's new command, how to stay, although he was the second last.

Even better, from my point of view, Travis was having trouble with his dog, a little black mutt. He got so mad that he yanked the dog's leash hard, right there in front of everyone. The dog yelped in pain. Maggie took the leash away from Travis. Mr. Weller took Travis over to one side of the room and talked to him. When Travis came back to get his dog, he still looked angry. He couldn't get his dog to do anything for the rest of the afternoon.

At the end of every session, we're all supposed to take our dogs back to their kennels. Travis hung back so that he was the last one out of the training room. He was still in the kennel after everyone else left. Maybe he noticed me there and maybe he didn't. He opened up the gate to his dog's kennel and kicked the dog. The dog yelped again.

"Hey," I said.

Travis turned on me. "Mind your own business, Gillick," he said.

"Then leave the dog alone. It didn't do anything," I said.

Travis banged the gate shut and shoved me, hard. I hate when people shove me around. I shoved him back as hard as I could. Then we really got into it. I probably would have slugged him if Scott hadn't seen us and hadn't run to get Mr. Weller.

Mr. Weller said, "Break it up." Boy, did he look mad.

I pulled away from Travis.

"What's going on?" Mr. Weller said.

"Are you gonna be like your friend?" Travis whispered to me. He meant Scott. "You gonna snitch on me?"

"Josh? I asked you a question. What's going on?" Mr. Weller said.

I looked at Travis. Then I looked at Scott. I wasn't like him.

"Nothing," I said.

Mr. Weller looked at me for a few seconds. It felt like a few hours. Finally he said, "Fighting isn't allowed. If I catch you fighting one more time, you're out of the program. Both of you."

It was only after they all left that the door to one of the kennels opened and Amy stepped out. She looked at me. She must have heard everything. But she didn't say a word.

I was on my way out to the parking lot when Mr. Weller caught up with me.

"Your brother just called, Josh," he said. "He has to work late. He can't pick you up. How about I give you a lift?"

"I can take the bus," I said. "But thanks anyway."

But Mr. Weller wouldn't take no for an answer.

I thought he was going to lecture me about fighting. He didn't. Instead he told me I was doing a good job with Sully. He said that the dogs in the program are used to being treated badly. But he said they can change with patience and kindness. He said people are the same way. He dropped me off at a corner near the apartment, right in front of a kitchen store. There was a display of mugs in the front window. I stared at Mr. Weller.

"I hear you had a little accident in the kitchen this morning," Mr. Weller said.

Miranda must have told Andrew. Andrew must have told Mr. Weller.

After Mr. Weller left, I went and looked in the store window. I saw a mug that looked a lot like Miranda's. It wasn't the exact same color, but it was blue, which was her favorite. I dug in my pocket. I hadn't spent most of the money I had made the week before delivering papers. I counted what I had. It was just enough.

"What's this?" Miranda said when I held out the bag.

"It's for you," I said.

She hooked the bag with one finger, like it was filled with dirty underwear or something. Then she opened it and looked inside. She looked so surprised I thought she was going to cry.

"I'm sorry I broke your mug," I said.

"I can't believe this," she said. "I can't believe you did something so thoughtful."

She couldn't believe it? What did she think I was? Some kind of monster? I could feel myself tense up inside. She didn't have to be *so* surprised.

Then I remembered what Mr. Weller had said. Miranda was used to me treating her like the enemy.

"I've been thinking," I said. "Maybe you and Andrew need some time alone together. I can babysit for you any time you want to go out. For free."

She smiled at me. Miranda actually smiled at me. Then she hugged me. It was the first time she had ever done that.

Chapter Nine

For a while things settled down. I went to school in the mornings. I went to the program in the afternoons. I concentrated on Sully. I didn't pay any attention to Travis, no matter how many times he needled me. I didn't pay any attention to Scott, either. If I had a problem with Sully, I went directly to Maggie.

Sully did great. He learned to stay. He learned to come. He learned not to jump up every time he got excited.

"You're doing outstanding work, Josh," Maggie said to me after one session. "Sully has really learned to trust you. Next week he'll learn to trust someone else."

"What do you mean?" I said.

Mr. Weller clapped his hands to get our attention.

"Next week," he said, "everyone switches dogs."

Everyone started talking at the same time. Most of us were complaining. Why did we have to switch dogs? Why couldn't we keep the dogs we had been working with? Mr. Weller had to do a lot of clapping to get our attention again.

"The reason you're working with these dogs is so that they can be adopted," he said. "You have all done good work with the dogs. They've learned a lot. But they have to learn to obey other people, not just you. That's why we're switching. So the dogs can learn to obey someone else."

A few people still grumbled, but not as many.

That night, for the first time since I had come to live with him, Andrew lost it. He was supposed to be putting Digby to bed while Miranda finished the dishes. But Digby just kept wailing. I heard Andrew yell at him. I heard something that sounded like a slap. For a moment it was silent. Then Digby let loose with the longest, loudest shriek I had ever heard.

Miranda ran into the bedroom. I heard her say, "What happened?" Then she said, "His bottom is all red. Did you hit him, Andrew?"

Andrew came out of the bedroom. Miranda ran after him. She was holding the baby, who had no clothes on. He was still crying.

"Did you, Andrew?" Miranda said. "Did you hit him?"

But Andrew was already out the door. Miranda glowered at me, like it was all my fault. She went back into the bedroom. I heard her talking softly to the baby. After a while, he stopped crying.

Andrew was gone for hours. Miranda sat in the living room watching TV with me, but I could tell that she wasn't really watching. She kept looking at the time. Finally, around ten o'clock, I said, "You want me to go and find him?"

"Do you know where he would be?"

"I have a few ideas," I said.

She nodded.

I found Andrew in the first place I looked—one of those pub-style restaurants near the apartment. He was sitting at the bar. I slid onto the stool next to him. When he looked at me, I saw his eyes were red. I looked at the glass in front of him and wondered how many he had had.

"Maybe you should have some coffee," I said. "Then we can go home. Miranda is worried."

"I can't believe I did that," he said. "I can't believe I hit my own kid." He took another sip of his drink.

"You've probably had enough," I said.

"What?"

"You've probably had enough to drink."

"It's soda water, Josh."

"Right."

He pushed the glass toward me. "Go on. Try it."

I did. It was soda water.

"I quit drinking," he said.

Andrew was a responsible guy. He was never late for work. But, boy, he liked to party on the weekends.

"You quit? When?"

"While you were away," he said. "As soon as I became a father."

I hadn't really been paying attention, but once he said that I realized that I hadn't seen him drink around the apartment. Not even a beer.

"How come?"

"I didn't want to turn out like Dad."

Our father used to drink a lot. Too much. He got mean when he drank. Then one night he got into his car when he shouldn't have and ended up wrapped around a concrete utility pole.

"I didn't want to ever hit my kids the way Dad used to hit us." His eyes got all watery. "You know what they say, Josh? They say people who were knocked around when they were kids grow up to knock their own kids around. I don't want to be like that."

I looked at him for a long time. My big brother.

"You know what else they say, Andrew?" I said. "People can change. Isn't that what you keep telling me? I can change? If I can change, you can turn out not to be anything like Dad."

We sat there for a while longer. He told me all about what it was like when Digby was born. How scared he'd been. How he was in awe of Miranda. She was so calm around the baby, and she always knew what to do. He finally agreed to come home with me. Miranda was so glad to see him that she started to cry. I heard them talking softly in the bedroom for a long time after that.

Chapter Ten

Travis got Sully.

I couldn't believe it.

Of all the people who could have ended up with Sully, Travis got him.

I got Amy's scared little dog.

"You have to talk soft to her," Amy said. "You can't shout at her." She looked worried.

"I'll be good to her, I promise," I told her.

Travis wasn't good to Sully, though. In fact, Travis came to the session in a rotten mood that day. He slouched in his chair and didn't participate at all. When Mr. Weller asked him how his weekend was, he just shrugged. Mr. Weller didn't push it. He never pushed it.

Sully wouldn't do anything for Travis. A couple of times I wanted to go over to Travis and tell him to calm down. But Mr. Weller came up to me and said, "They both have to learn, Josh." So I let it go.

Travis was in an even worse mood the next day. He was impatient with Sully the whole time. Sully responded by not listening and not doing anything right. Some of the kids jazzed Travis about it, but that only made him angrier and more impatient. After the session, he shoved Sully into his kennel and then banged on the gate. That got Sully all riled up. Travis smiled at that.

I caught up with him at the bus stop. There were five or six other kids there, kids who didn't get rides and who were waiting for the bus.

"Hey," I said to Travis. "If you've got a problem, don't take it out on the dog."

"Yeah?" Travis said. "Or what?"

"Or you'll have to answer to me," I said.

Travis laughed. "You're scaring me, Gillick," he said.

My hands clenched into fists at my side. Everyone was watching us.

"Leave the dog alone, Travis. I mean it."

He laughed again. "You're a wuss," he said. "You won't touch me."

I stared at him.

He turned to look at the other kids who were waiting for the bus. "You know Scott?" he said. "Scott and Gillick were friends. Then Scott turned Gillick in." He looked at me. "That's the way it happened, isn't it, Gillick? Your friend Scott ratted you out to the cops, right?"

I hit him.

I knew it was wrong when I was doing it, but I hit him.

Hard.

I knocked him right over.

I probably would have hit him again if Amy hadn't grabbed my arm and pulled me away—well, she tried to. She's pretty small.

"He's not worth it," she said. "You'll get kicked out of the program."

Then Mr. Weller was there, asking what had happened. Where had he come from? Why was he up at the bus stop? He didn't take the bus. He drove here.

I couldn't look at him.

He asked Travis. Travis looked directly at me when he answered. He said, "Nothing."

Mr. Weller stared at him a minute. Then he turned to me.

"What happened, Josh?"

"Nothing," I said. "It was nothing."

"I warned you once, Josh. You too, Travis. You're both this close to getting kicked out of the program." He looked at me a minute longer. Then he walked back toward the shelter.

"Your friend Scott is trying hard to get rid of you," Travis said.

"Scott? What does he have to do with anything?"

Travis nodded back to the shelter. Mr. Weller was going up the main walk now. Scott was standing just outside the door.

"He doesn't know how to mind his own business," Travis said. "He saw you hit me, and he snitched on you. Again."

I looked back at Scott. He came across so nice and helpful to everyone in the program. They didn't know him like I did.

The phone rang around 9:00. It was for Andrew. He listened more than he talked. Then he said, "Sure. I understand. I'll talk to him."

When he got off the phone, he came into the living room where Miranda was watching TV. I was doing my homework at the table.

"That was Brian Weller," Andrew said. He looked mad. "He said you hit some guy today. Is that true?"

"The guy was hurting one of the dogs."

"So you hit him?" The way Andrew said it made it sound like even if Travis had killed a dog, I shouldn't touch him.

"The guy is a jerk, Andrew. He hurts the dogs and he's always needling me."

"That's no excuse," Andrew said. But he didn't stop there. He kept right on going. He said it didn't sound like I was making much progress if I hit someone and then wasn't even sorry about it. He said I should apologize to the guy. He said I should be grateful that Mr. Weller was giving me a second chance. When I tried to explain again what happened, he said he didn't want to hear it. Boy, Scott just never stopped getting me in trouble—first with the cops, then with Mr. Weller and now with Andrew.

"What did I tell you about following the rules, Josh?" Andrew said.

That's when I left the apartment. I had to get out of there. I had to get some air.

Chapter Eleven

Andrew shook me awake the next morning. He kept his voice low when he said, "Where were you last night, Josh?"

I had already told him that when I got back to the apartment and found him sitting in the living room waiting for me.

"I was walking around," I said. "Trying to calm down."

"The cops are here," he said. "They want to talk to you."

"Cops? What for?"

"They're in the kitchen. Get dressed, Josh."

There were two of them, a man and a woman. They were sitting at the table, drinking coffee that Miranda must have made for them. The woman cop said they wanted to ask me some questions. She said I didn't have to answer anything if I didn't want to, but if I said anything, they could use it against me. She asked me if I understood that. I said I did. She said it was okay for Andrew to be there if I wanted him. I said I did.

"Are you charging him with something?" Andrew asked.

"We just want to ask a few questions," the woman cop said. "Where were you last night around 10:00, Josh?"

"I was out walking around."

"Where?"

"Just around."

"Do you know Scott Alexander?"

Scott? Did this have something to do with him?

"Yeah," I said. "Why?"

"He was attacked last night. In a park not far from here."

"Is he okay?"

"He's in the hospital. He's unconscious."

Jeez.

"How do you know him?" the woman cop said.

"We used to be friends," I said. "We used to do stuff together."

"You and Scott Alexander used to snatch purses together, is that right?" the woman cop's partner said.

I hated to think about that. "Yeah," I said.

"And after the last time, he went to the police and turned you in, is that right?"

The last time. I hated to think about that too. That last time, everything went wrong. The woman we picked out just wouldn't let go of her purse. I couldn't believe it. Most women get scared when two guys come at them. But this one held tight. I got so mad I hit her with the weighted wooden priest that used to belong to my dad. Hit her in the wrong place. Too hard. She crumpled to the ground. I grabbed her purse and we ran.

It turned out she had a good reason for not letting go. Her purse was filled with cash—more than five thousand dollars. We read in the paper later that it was money she had raised for AIDS research. Her brother had died of AIDS. When Scott heard that, he almost started to cry.

"We have to give it back," he said. He said it over and over.

I told him he was crazy.

Scott told me he was going to the cops. He asked me to go with him.

I said no. I said he could go if he wanted to, but no way was I going to turn myself in and no way was I giving back the money.

I thought that was the end of it.

Until Scott ratted me out.

"I heard you ran into him again recently," the woman cop said. "He got you into trouble again, didn't he? Because of him, you could get thrown out of the program you're in, and then you'll be in trouble with your youth worker. Isn't that right?"

Wait a minute. "Are you saying *I* hurt Scott?"

The man cop pulled something out of his pocket. It was a photograph.

"You recognize this, Josh?"

I stared at it. It couldn't be.

Andrew looked at it too. After a moment he said, "That looks like the fish club Dad gave you."

"Those are your initials, aren't they, Josh?" the woman cop said.

I nodded.

"It's what Scott was hit with. We have it down at the police station, Josh. Besides your initials, it has your fingerprints on it."

"That can't be right," I said. "It's right here. It's in my box."

They let me look for it, even though it turned out they knew I wouldn't find it. It wasn't there. It wasn't in the box. It wasn't under the couch. It wasn't anywhere.

But they didn't arrest me. They said they were going to talk to Scott first. They warned Andrew to keep a close eye on me.

Chapter Twelve

"I didn't do it," I told Andrew.

He just nodded. He didn't say he believed me. Miranda didn't say anything at all.

I went to school because I had to, but I can't remember anything either of my teachers said that day.

Then I went to the program because I had to. I thought Mr. Weller would give me a hard time, but he didn't. He told everyone that Scott wouldn't be in that day, but he didn't say why. He didn't press me to talk in circle, either.

Amy's little dog, Coco, was pretty good that day, which was good because I didn't need any hassle. I just wanted the program to be over.

As soon as we were finished, I headed for the bus stop. I stood apart from the others who were taking the bus, and when the bus came, I took a seat in the very back.

Amy dropped down in the seat next to me.

"Are you okay?" she said.

"Sure," I said.

"Because you're really quiet today," she said.

I stayed quiet.

"Did you hear what they're saying about Scott?" she said. "They're saying he's in the hospital. They're saying someone beat him up."

I stayed quiet.

"I heard Travis say you and Scott were

friends," she said."You want to go see him?"

"What?" If she had heard Travis, then she also knew what Scott had done to me.

"Your friend is hurt. You want to go and see him?"

I noticed then that she had light blue eyes. They stared right at me, almost like she knew me.

"I'll go with you if you want," she said.

I didn't say anything.

"I got into a fight with my best friend," she said. "It wasn't her fault. I was mad because of stuff at home and she said something and I started hitting her. She ended up in the hospital. That's why I'm in the program. I'm supposed to learn how to control my anger."

"I didn't hurt Scott," I said. "And we're not exactly friends anymore."

"I know," she said. "So, you want to go and see him?"

"What is it with you?" I said. "Why do you even care?"

She shrugged. "Why shouldn't I?"

The truth was, yeah, I wanted to go to the hospital. I wanted to see Scott. I wanted to tell him that it wasn't me. But I didn't think they'd let me get near him. Amy said, "You'll never know until you try."

Amy was the one who went to the information desk to ask what room Scott was in. She told the woman she was Scott's girlfriend. When we got upstairs, I froze and ducked back around a corner.

"What's the matter?" Amy said.

"That woman who just came out of that room? That's Scott's mother."

She peeked around the corner.

"She's down by the elevator. Maybe she's leaving. Or going for coffee or something."

"Let's get out of here," I said.

"You came to see him. So go see him. I'll wait by the door and let you know if anyone is coming."

I shook my head.

"Come on, Josh," she said. "You're a good guy. I know it."

There were those blue eyes again, looking right into me. Then she took my hand and led me to Scott's room as if I was a little kid. She pushed me inside.

"I'll let you know when anyone comes," she said.

Scott's eyes were closed, but he opened them when I came into the room. He had one black eye and a huge bandage on his head.

"Hey," he said.

"Hey. How are you feeling?"

He smiled just a little and then winced. "I've got a really bad headache," he said.

"Are you going to be okay?"

"I think so. They said I have a concussion and they want to watch me for a while. But they're not acting weird, like I'm dying or anything. And I haven't forgotten anything. At least, I don't think I have." There was that goofy grin again. If he could grin like that, I figured he'd be okay.

I tried to think of what to say to him. Finally I just said what I had told the cops and Andrew.

"I know I was mad at you for snitching on me," I said. "To the cops and at the shelter. But I just wanted you to know, it wasn't me, Scott."

He started to grin again. I couldn't tell if he believed me. Then he said, "Hey, Josh, I—"

"Josh!"

I turned and saw Amy in the doorway.

"We better go," she said. "His mother's coming back. And there's cops with her."

I got out of there fast. I saw Scott's mother and the cops down at the nurses' station. They were talking to one of the nurses. I don't think they saw us. We took off down the stairs and kept right on going until we were a couple of blocks from the hospital.

"Did you say what you wanted to say?" Amy asked.

"Yeah." Then I said something else I wanted to say. "Thanks."

Chapter Thirteen

Miranda was pacing up and down in the kitchen when I came through the door. She was holding Digby in her arms. He wasn't wearing a sleeper like he usually did around the house. Miranda had dressed him in a T-shirt and a pair of little baby jeans. She was more dressed up than usual too.

"Are you going out?" I said.

"The police phoned. They want you to go down to the police station."

I felt sick, like someone had punched me in the stomach.

"Andrew can't get off work. He said I should go with you."

"Are they going to arrest me?"

"They just said they wanted to talk to you and that you should come down there." She picked up Digby's diaper bag and grabbed her keys. "We're going to have to take the bus."

She didn't say anything all the way to the police station. When we got there, she asked for a police officer by name. It was the woman cop again. She showed us into a room and said she wanted to ask some more questions. She said Miranda could stay if I wanted her there.

"He does," Miranda said before I could answer. I guessed that Andrew had told her she had to stay with me. She settled Digby on her lap.

The woman cop put my wooden priest onto the table.

"Remember I said we found this in the park where Scott Alexander was beaten up?" she said. I nodded. "Is it yours?"

I stared at it. It was mine. Even without the initials I would have recognized it. It was beat up in a few places—it had been for as long as I could remember.

"Did you take it to the park, Josh?"

"No."

"Do you have any idea how it got to the park?"

"No."

"The only fingerprints on it are yours," she said. "Can you explain that?"

"It's his," Miranda said. "Of course his fingerprints are on it."

"I meant, if he isn't the one who hit Scott Alexander with it, why aren't there other fingerprints on it?" the woman cop said. She said it nicely, though. "When was the last time you saw it, Josh?"

"I—I can't remember. A couple of weeks ago, maybe."

"Did you take it somewhere and lose it?"

I looked at her. The questions weren't the ones I expected.

"No," I said. "I never take it out of the house. It's always in my room—" I broke off. It wasn't *my* room. "It's always in the living room. That's where I sleep. I keep it in a crate in the living room."

"So as far as you know, it's never been outside of the apartment?" the woman cop said. She sounded disappointed.

"That's right," I said.

"Josh, do you own a leather jacket?" the cop said.

"No," Miranda answered for me.

The cop looked at her. "We can check."

"He doesn't own a leather jacket," Miranda said. "Why?"

The cop looked directly at me.

"Scott says he didn't see the guy who attacked him. He says the guy grabbed him from behind, but he could tell he was wearing a leather jacket. He says he tried to get the guy off him. He slammed him backward into the cement wall that runs around the side of the park. You know that wall, Josh?"

I nodded. I could picture it.

"He says he rammed the guy into the wall and then tried to pull away. He says he could hear the guy's leather jacket scrape against the wall before the guy started hitting him with that." She nodded at the priest, but she was looking directly at me. "The jacket must have got scraped pretty bad," she said. "If you look closely, you can see traces of leather on the wall."

"Josh doesn't have a leather jacket," Miranda said again.

"Did you borrow the jacket from someone, Josh?"

What? "No."

"But this is your weapon. And the only fingerprints on it are yours. And you were mad at Scott. And you were out that night when you should have been at home. Is that right?"

"I didn't do it," I said.

"So this thing just walked itself down to the park, attached itself to someone wearing a leather jacket and beat up Scott Alexander? Is that what you're saying, Josh? It just walked out of the apartment by itself?"

"I took it outside," Miranda said quietly. The cop looked at her. "Josh leaves his stuff lying around, even when I tell him to put it away. I get mad. I tell him if he doesn't pick up after himself, I'll pick everything up and throw it out." She glanced at me, then looked back at the cop. "I put Josh's box of things outside in the hall once. And out back near the dumpster another time."

The cop nodded. "How long ago was that?"

"I don't know. A week. A week and a half maybe."

"And what happened to it?" the cop said.

"I saw the crate when I got home. I brought it back upstairs."

"Was the priest in it then?"

I shook my head. "I don't know. I didn't check."

The cop looked at Miranda. "Did you see anyone look at the box or go near the box?"

"No," Miranda said. "I mean, I didn't check on it or anything. I just left it there. I was pretty mad." Then she frowned. "But there were some kids hanging around out back when I went out with it."

"Kids?" the cop said.

"Some teenagers who live in the building." She looked at me. "That boy who lives at the end of the hall and some of his friends."

Oh.

Both the cop and Miranda were staring at me.

I stared down at the table.

"You want to know what else Scott Alexander told me, Josh?" the cop said. "He told me he doesn't think you'd be stupid enough to attack him and then leave the weapon right there where someone would find it. Especially that weapon. But he said if you had an idea who did it, you just might be stupid enough to try to handle it yourself instead of snitching to the cops. Is that right, Josh? Because if it is, you could end up in even more trouble."

"Josh, do you know who did it?" Miranda said.

I looked at her and at Digby, who was being so good on her lap.

"He was badly hurt, Josh," the cop said. "And whoever did it to him should be held accountable. It's the right thing to do. Scott said to tell you it's what he would do."

I pictured Scott saying that. I pictured his goofy smile when he said it.

"Josh," Miranda said. "You should tell."

Chapter Fourteen

"Jeez, Miranda, stop, would you?" I said. She had fussed at my hair before we left the apartment. She had fussed at my shirt collar before we got into the car. Now that we were in the parking lot at the shelter, she was tugging at the stupid tie I was wearing.

"I just want to straighten it, Josh," she said. "I want you to look good. Andrew is going to take pictures."

All of the kids in the program had brought someone with them—a parent, two parents, a guardian, a foster parent. They all looked a lot neater than they normally did and were all wearing their good clothes. Amy was wearing a skirt and a clingy top. She looked amazing. She was with a woman who looked exactly like her, only older. She introduced us—the woman was her mother—and I introduced both of them to Andrew, Miranda and Digby. Scott was there too.

The only person who was missing was Travis. The cops had arrested him. It turned out his cool leather jacket was all scraped in the back from where Scott had dragged it against the wall. He wasn't locked up, but he was in a group home again where he would get close supervision. He wasn't allowed to continue in the program.

Mr. Weller started to clap his hands to get everyone's attention. He talked about the program and what it was supposed to accomplish, both for the dogs and for the kids. Then he said he wanted the guests to judge for themselves how well we had done. He nodded at Scott, who pulled down a movie screen and turned off the lights.

They played the video from the second day. I remembered that I had been scared the first few times I met Sully, but I was surprised by how scared everyone else looked. I was surprised, too, by how badly behaved the dogs were. They were all jumping and barking and pulling in every direction. Then the camera focused on me making Sully sit. Miranda gasped when Sully lunged at me. Everyone except Miranda laughed when I jumped back fast and stepped on Amy's dog's tail.

"They made you work with that vicious dog?" Miranda said. She sounded shocked.

"He's not vicious," I said.

After the video, the kids in the program all went out of the room. When we came back, we had our dogs on leashes. The dogs all walked to heel. None of them barked or jumped. The people in the audience looked sort of stunned, as if they couldn't believe these were the same dogs.

One by one, Mr. Weller called us to the middle of the room. One by one, we showed how well our dogs listened to and obeyed commands. I got Sully to sit, stay, come when called, roll over and shake a paw. Miranda clapped the loudest at the end of his performance.

"You worked wonders with that dog, Josh," she said.

"Yeah. Good work, Josh," Andrew said.

We all got a certificate that said we had completed the program and another certificate that said we had successfully passed a dog-training course. Mr. Weller told everyone that most of the dogs had been successfully adopted and would soon be leaving for their new homes. He came up to me after and said that Sully was one of the first to have found a home.

"He's going to a nice family, Josh," he said. "A nice young couple with a little boy." He smiled at Andrew, Miranda and Digby. "It looks to me like you and Sully have a lot in common."

He was right.

"They're always looking for volunteers here at the shelter," Mr. Weller said. "If you want me to, I can put in a word for you. And you never know," he added. "Sometimes volunteering leads to a job. Scott started here as a volunteer."

"I already filled out an application," I told him. "Scott helped me. I'm going to start next week." I looked at Andrew. "It's just twice a week," I said. "I'll also look for a job, I promise."

"I know you will, Josh," Andrew said. "So, you want to go get a burger or something to celebrate?"

I said I thought that would be great. Then I said, "Can Scott come too?"

OTHER TITLES IN THE ORCA SOUNDINGS SERIES

More Orca Soundings

Home Invasion
by Monique Polak

I was turning the corner to my street when I spotted the key. Someone had left it right in the lock of their front door. I walked up the front stairs and raised my finger to the doorbell. My plan was to let whoever lived there know they'd forgotten the key.

I didn't ring the doorbell. I turned the doorknob and let myself in.

Josh is less than thrilled that he has a new step-father and finds his personal habits—and his personality—irritating. Resenting his new living arrangements and his unorthodox home life, Josh finds himself drawn to the idea of a "regular" family and, on a whim, sneaks into a neighbor's house to see how others live. Considering it a harmless pastime, Josh continues entering people's houses until he is witness to a violent home invasion. Josh must use all his courage to save himself and bring the home invader to justice.

More Orca Soundings

Yellow Line
by Sylvia Olsen

Where I come from, kids are divided into two groups. White kids on one side; Indians, or First Nations, on the other. Sides of the room, sides of the field, the smoking pit, the hallway, the washrooms; you name it. We're on one side, and they're on the other. They live on one side of the Forks River bridge, and we live on the other side. They hang out in their village, and we hang out in ours.

Vince lives in a small town—a town that is divided right down the middle. Indians on one side, whites on the other. The unspoken rule has been there as long as Vince remembers, and no one challenges it. But when Vince's friend Sherry starts seeing an Indian boy, Vince is outraged and determined to fight back—until he notices Raedawn, a girl from the reserve. Trying to balance his community's prejudices with his shifting alliances, Vince is forced to take a stand and see where his heart will lead him.

Breathless
by Pam Withers

And the thing about panicking when you're forty feet under the ocean's surface is that you can drown, and you know you can drown. In fact, you can't breathe without your regulator even if you're not panicking. You're also not supposed to hold your breath, because there's pressure underwater. That means if you're not breathing out bubbles while the regulator is out, your chest might expand until it explodes.

Beverly is in Hawaii, helping her uncle at his dive shop, learning how to dive and trying to lose weight and get a boyfriend. When Garth, an accomplished diver, shows an interest in her, Beverly is ecstatic, until it turns out Garth is only interested in one thing. Struggling with failing strength from her self-imposed starvation diet, Beverly finds herself in deep trouble when she has to fight Garth off underwater.